EASY PIANO ARRANGEMENTS BY DAN COATES

© 2005 ALFRED PUBLISHING CO., INC.
All Rights Reserved

The Gift

Words and Music by
JIM BRICKMAN and TOM DOUGLAS
Arranged by DAN COATES

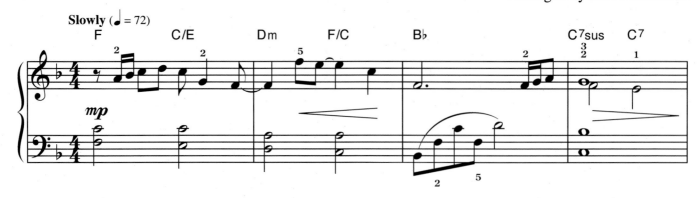

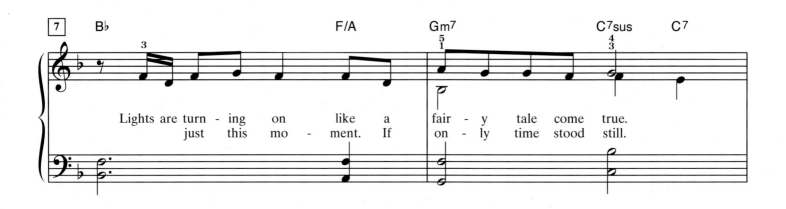

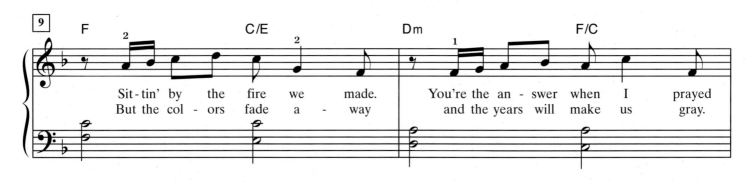

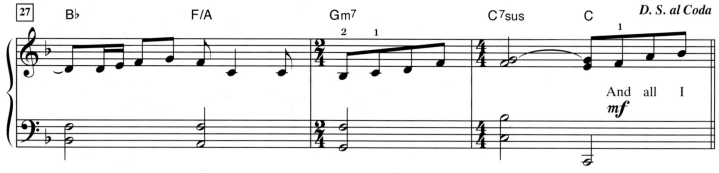

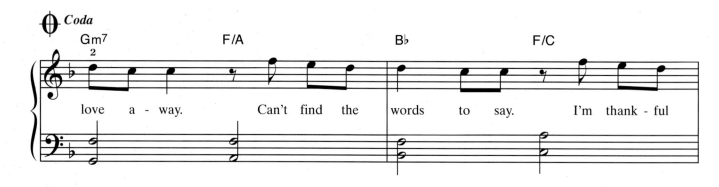

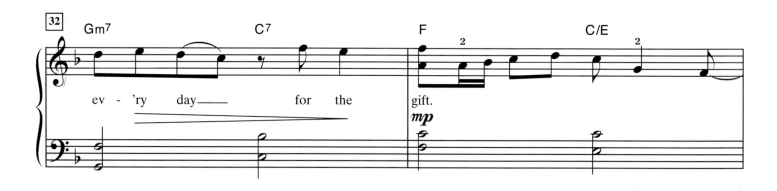

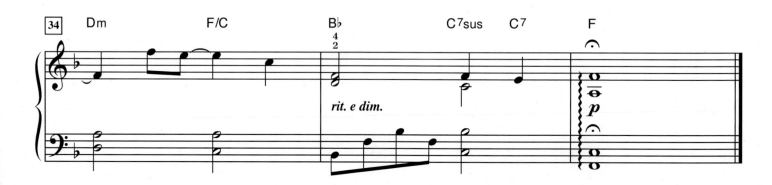

Thirty-Two Feet and Eight Little Tails

(Dasher, Dancer, Prancer, Vixen, Comet, Cupid, Donner, Blitzen)

Words and Music by
JOHN REDMOND, JAMES CAVANAUGH
and FRANK WELDON
Arranged by DAN COATES

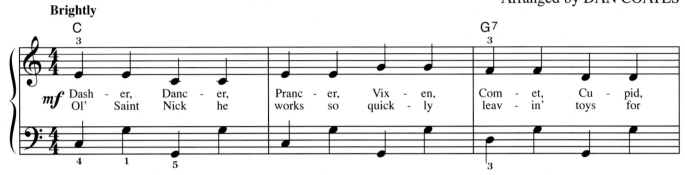

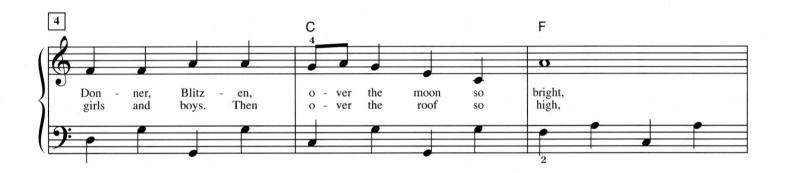

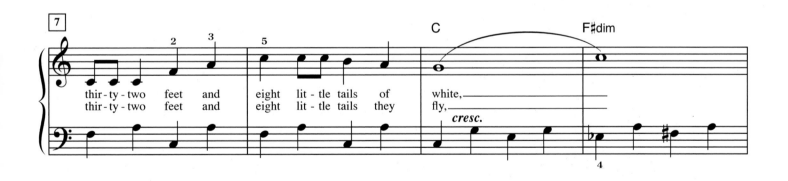

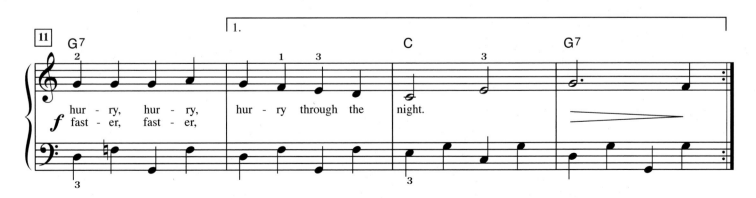

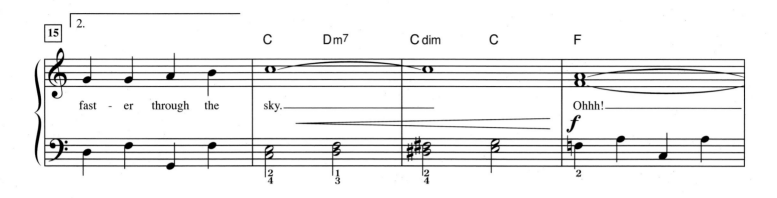

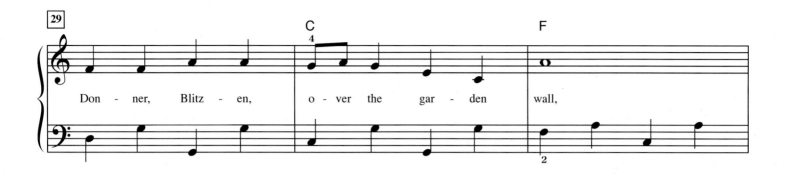

Don - ner, Blitz - en, o - ver the gar - den wall,

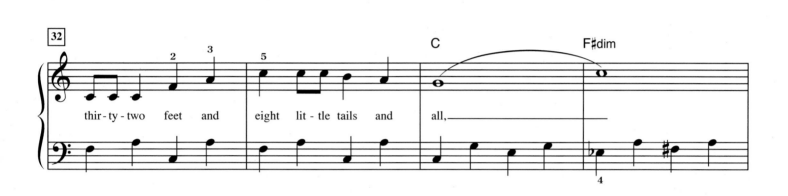

thir - ty - two feet and eight lit - tle tails and all,

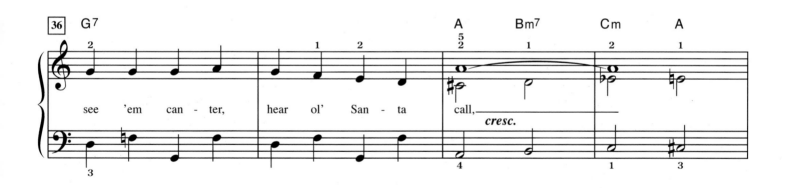

see 'em can - ter, hear ol' San - ta call, *cresc.*

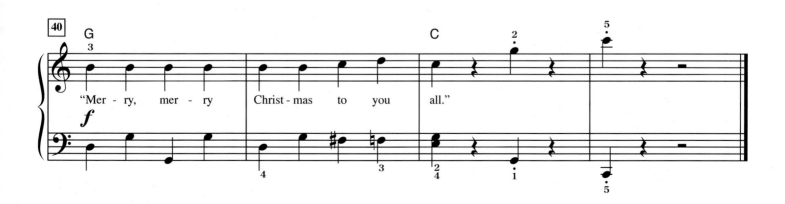

"Mer - ry, mer - ry Christ - mas to you all."

Jingle Bells

Words and Music by
JAMES PIERPONT
Arranged by DAN COATES

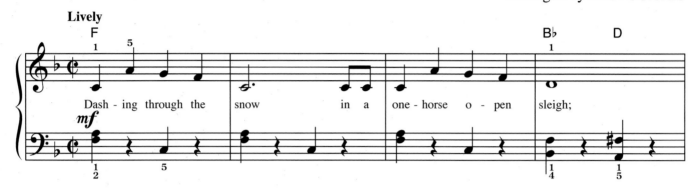

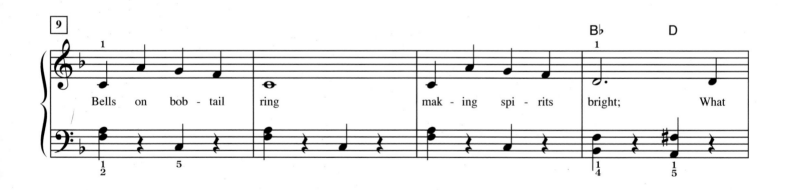

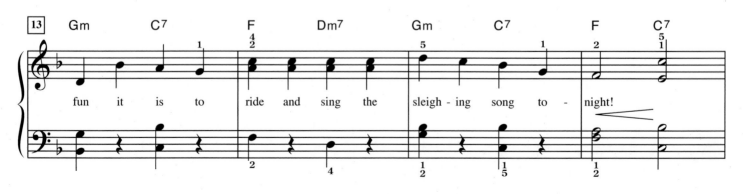

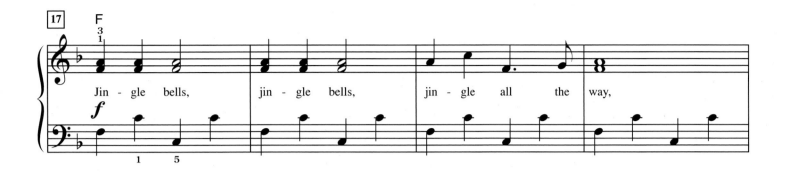

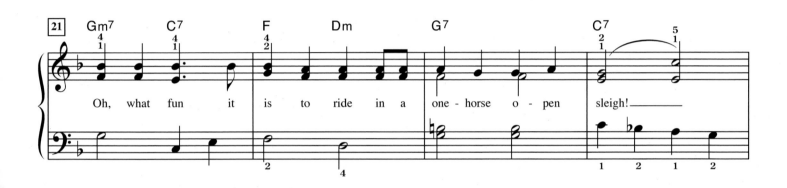

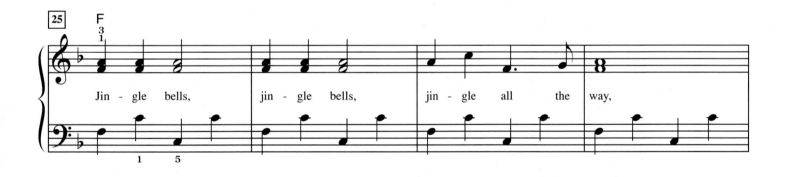

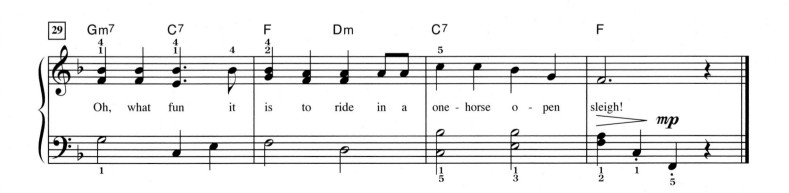

It Wouldn't Be Christmas Without You

By SCOTT KRIPPAYNE
and JOHN TESH
Arranged by DAN COATES

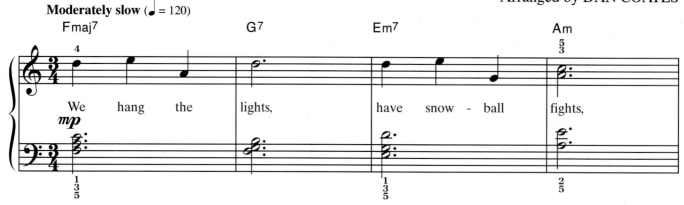

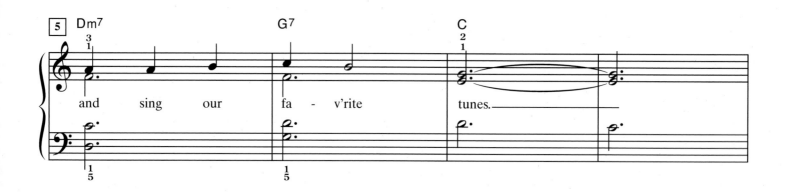

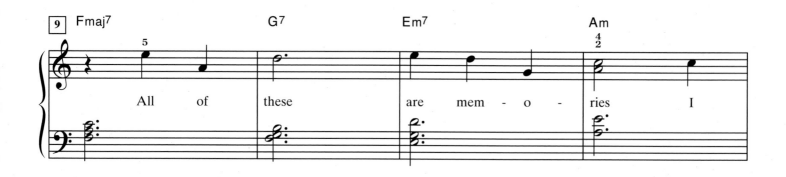

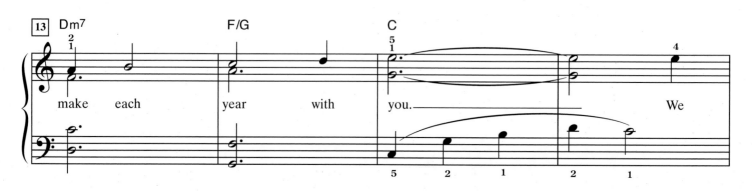

We Wish You a Merry Christmas

TRADITIONAL ENGLISH FOLK SONG
Arranged by DAN COATES

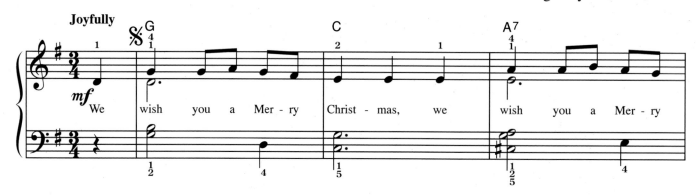

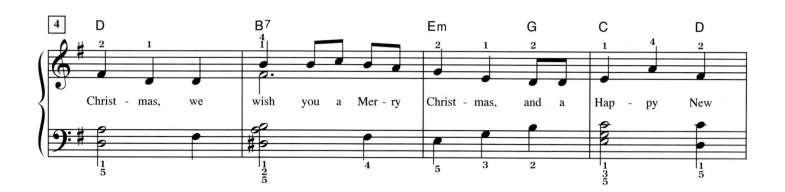

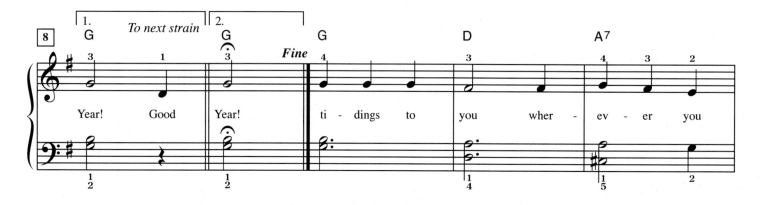

(There's No Place Like)
Home for the Holidays

Music by ROBERT ALLEN
Words by AL STILLMAN
Arranged by DAN COATES

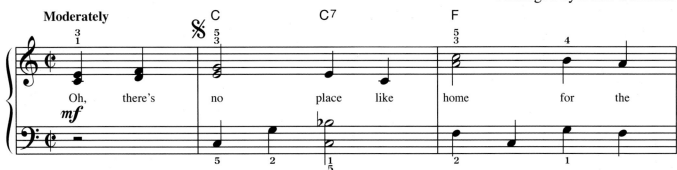

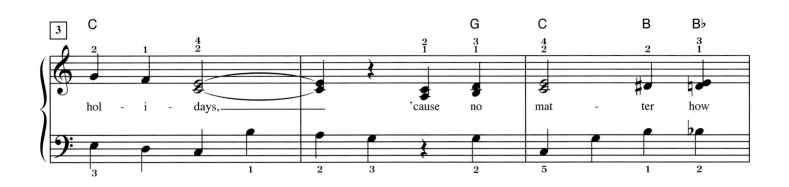

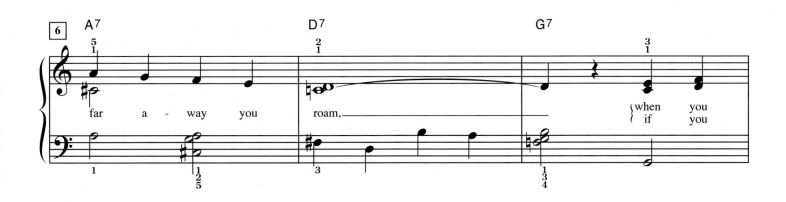

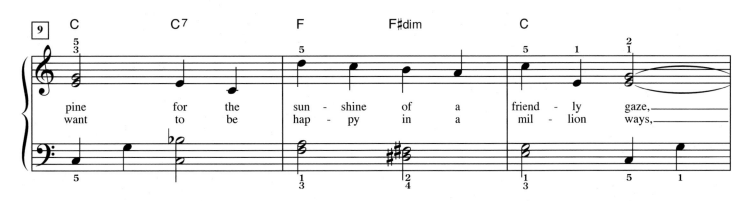

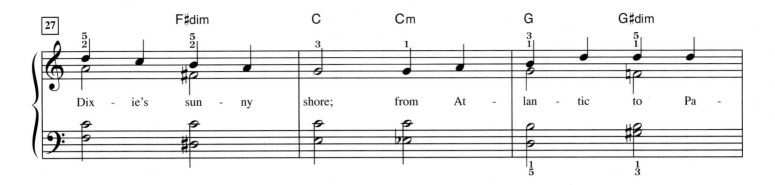

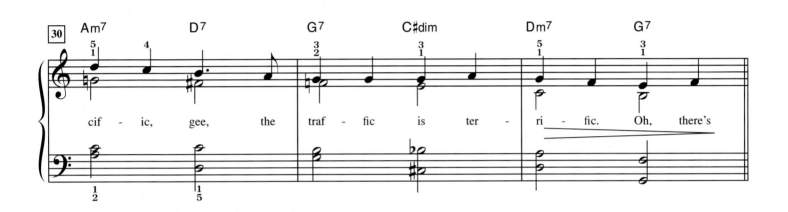

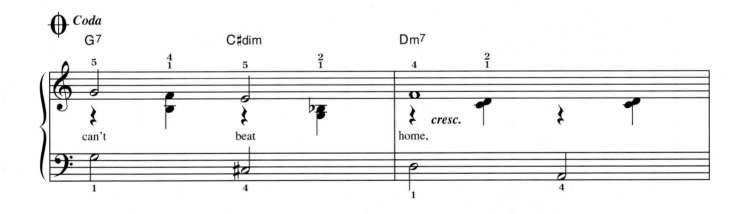

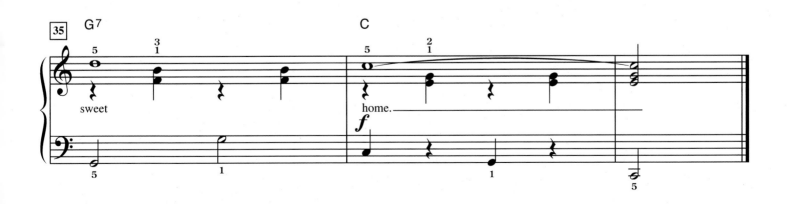

Let It Snow! Let It Snow! Let It Snow!

Music by JULE STYNE
Words by SAMMY CAHN
Arranged by DAN COATES

Who Comes This Night

Words by SALLY STEVENS
Music by DAVE GRUSIN
Arranged by DAN COATES

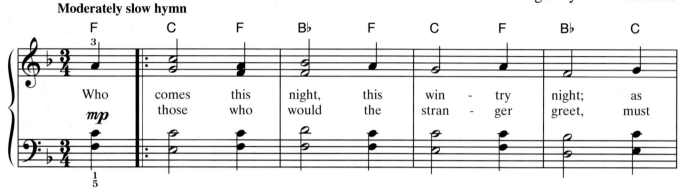

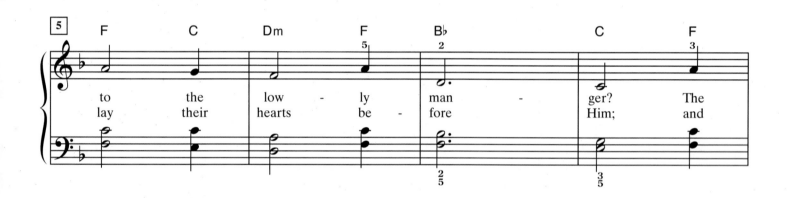

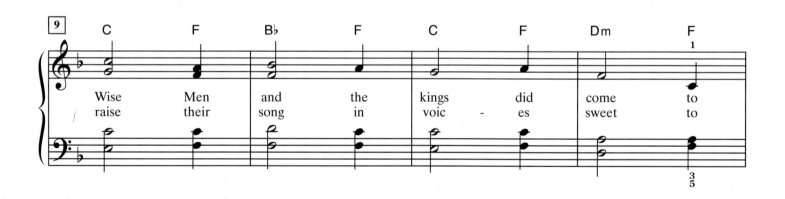

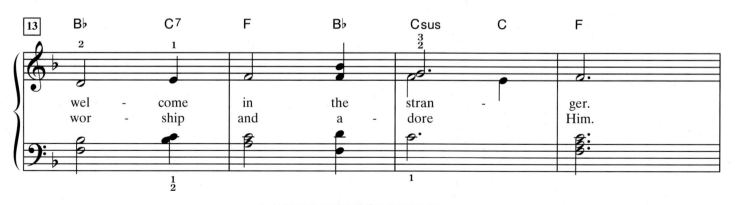

Nuttin' for Christmas

Words and Music by
SID TEPPER and ROY C. BENNETT
Arranged by DAN COATES

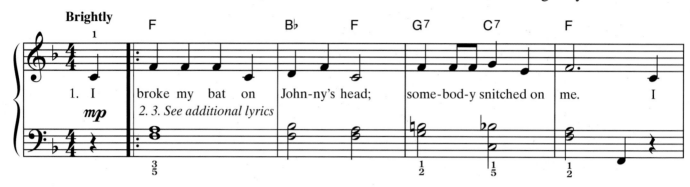

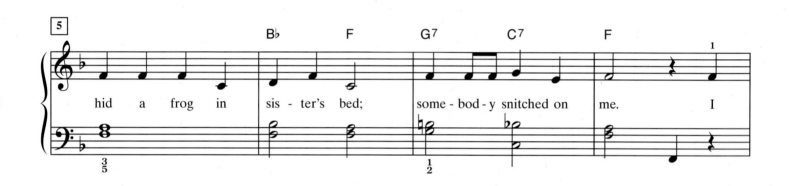

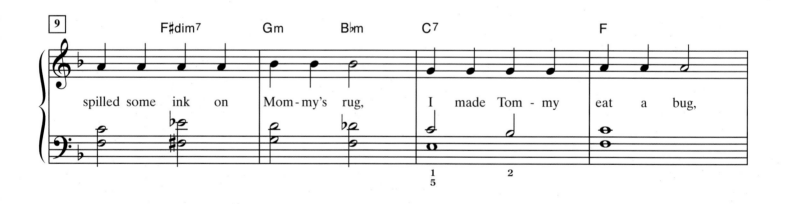

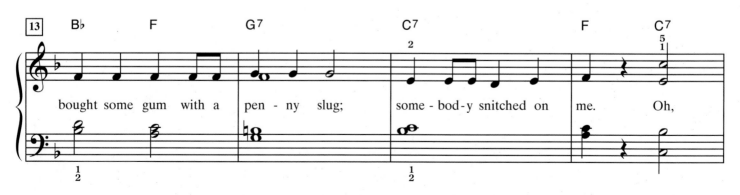

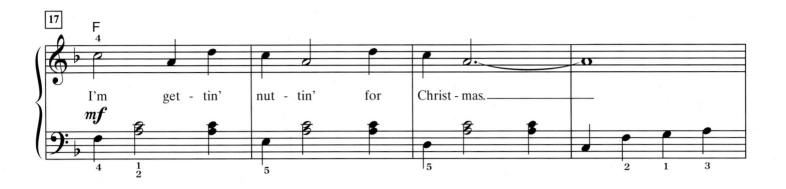

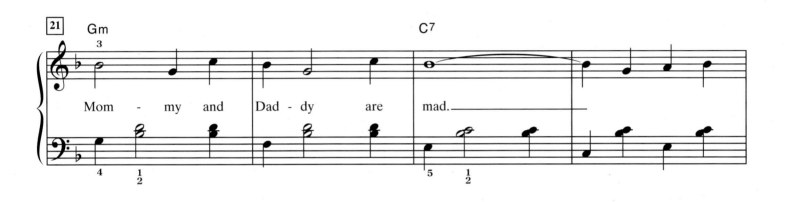

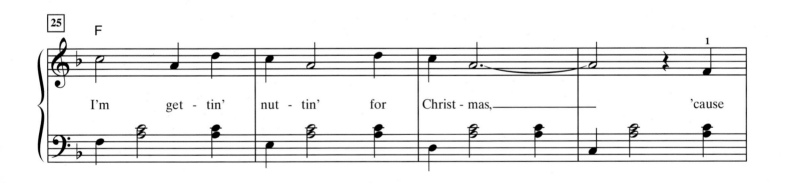

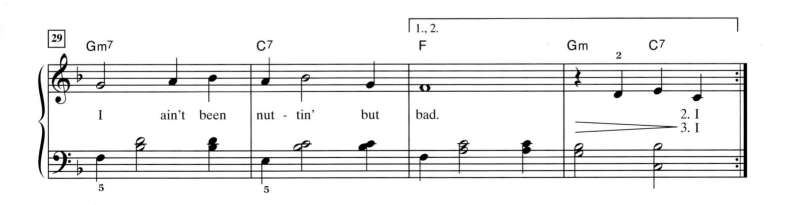

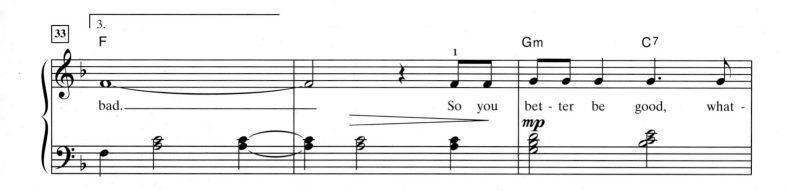

33 *3.*
F ... Gm ... C7

bad. So you bet - ter be good, what -

mp

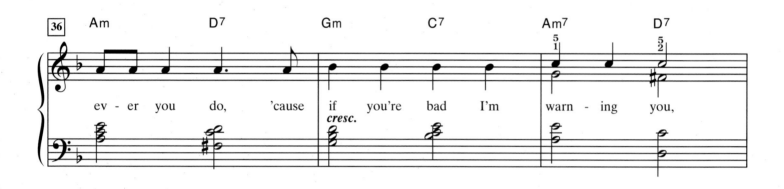

36 Am ... D7 ... Gm ... C7 ... Am7 ... D7

ev - er you do, 'cause if you're bad I'm warn - ing you,

cresc.

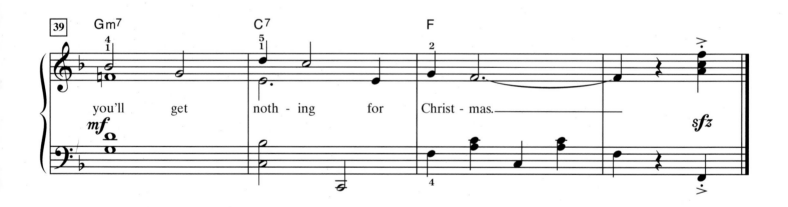

39 Gm7 ... C7 ... F

you'll get noth - ing for Christ - mas.

mf ... *sfz*

Verse 2:
I put a tack on teacher's chair;
Somebody snitched on me.
I tied a knot in Susie's hair;
Somebody snitched on me.
I did a dance on Mommy's plants,
Climbed a tree and tore my pants,
Filled the sugar bowl with ants;
Somebody snitched on me.
(To Chorus:)

Verse 3:
I won't be seeing Santa Claus;
Somebody snitched on me.
He won't come visit me because
Somebody snitched on me.
Next year I'll be going straight,
Next year I'll be good, just wait.
I'd start now but it's too late;
Somebody snitched on me.
(To Chorus:)

Frosty the Snowman

Words and Music by
STEVE NELSON and JACK ROLLINS
Arranged by DAN COATES

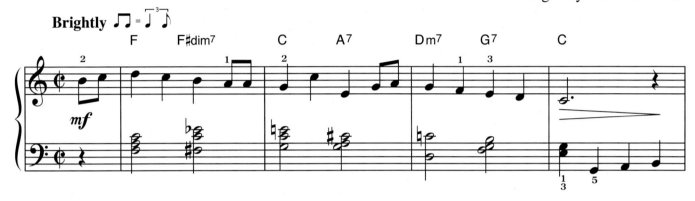

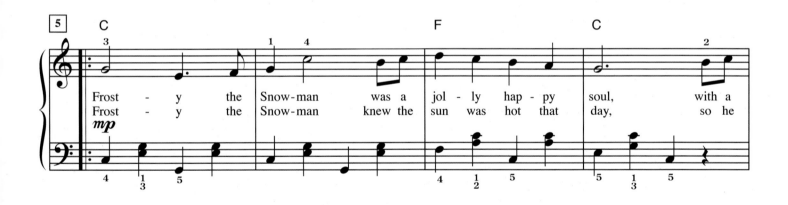

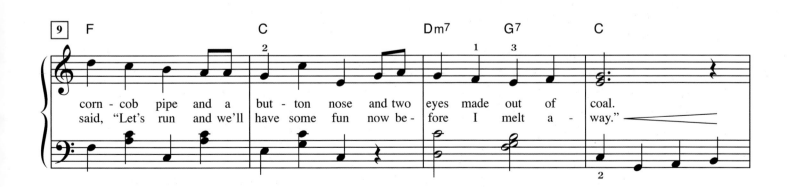

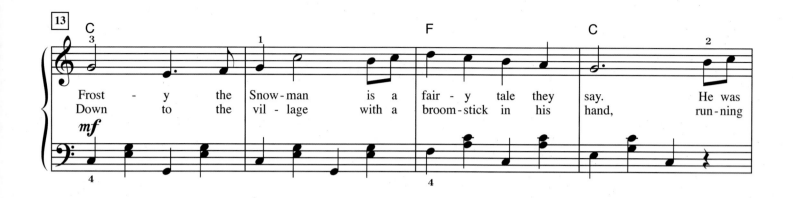

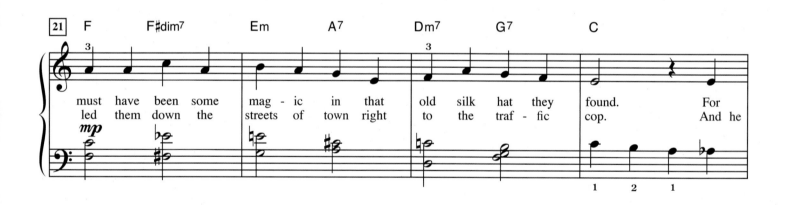

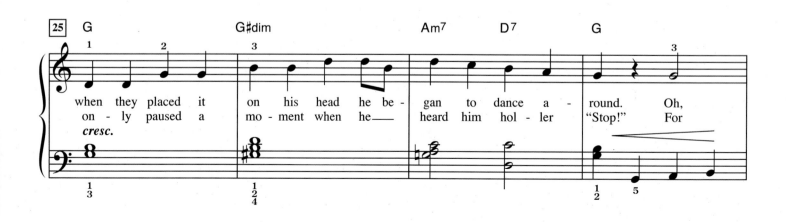

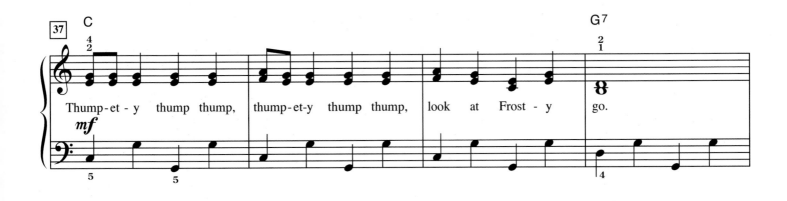

Don't Save It All for Christmas Day

Words and Music by
PETER ZIZZO, RIC WAKE
and CELINE DION
Arranged by DAN COATES

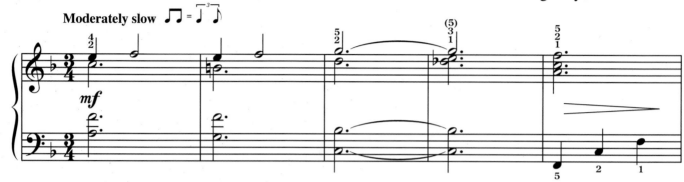

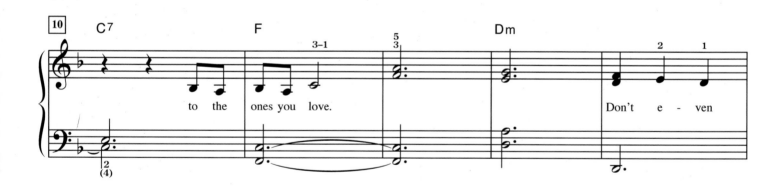

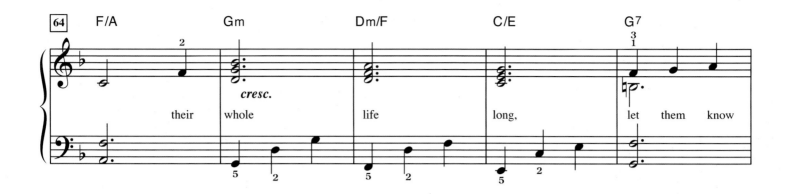

their whole life long, let them know

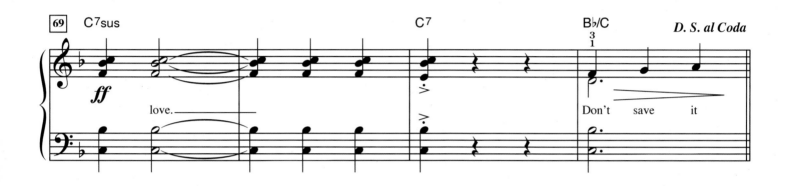

love. Don't save it

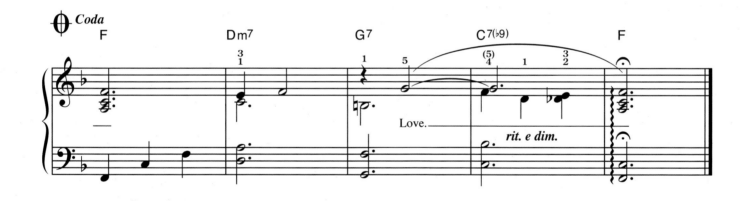

Love.

Verse 2:
How could you wait another minute,
A hug is warmer when you're in it.
And, baby, that's a fact.
And saying I love you's always better,
Seasons, reasons, they don't matter.
So don't hold back.
How many people in this world,
So needful in this world?
How many people are praying for love?
(To Chorus:)

I'll Be Home for Christmas

Words by KIM GANNON
Music by WALTER KENT
Arranged by DAN COATES

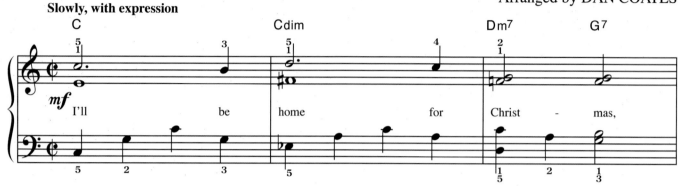

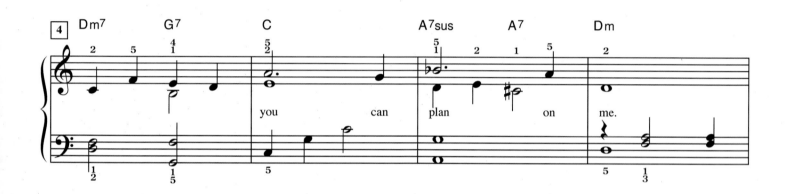

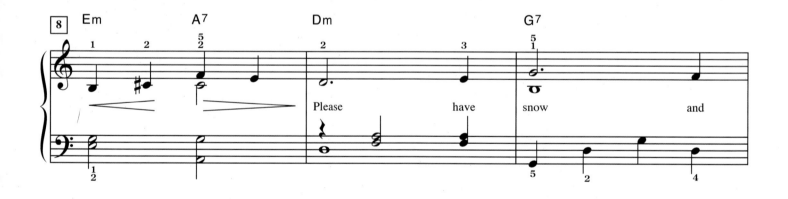

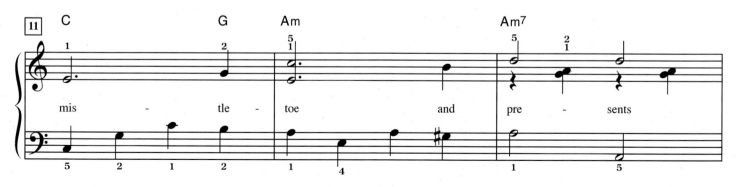

Grandma Got Run Over by a Reindeer

Words and Music by
RANDY BROOKS
Arranged by DAN COATES

Moderately bright

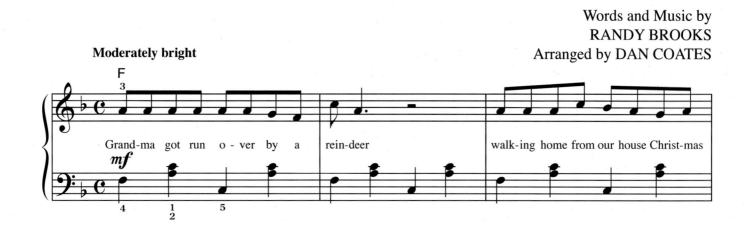

Grand-ma got run o-ver by a rein-deer walk-ing home from our house Christ-mas

Eve. You can say there's no such thing as San - ta, but

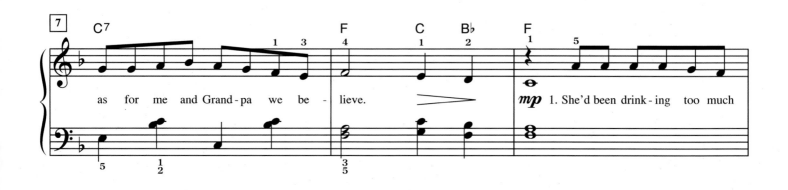

as for me and Grand-pa we be - lieve. 1. She'd been drink-ing too much

egg - nog—— and we begged her not to go,

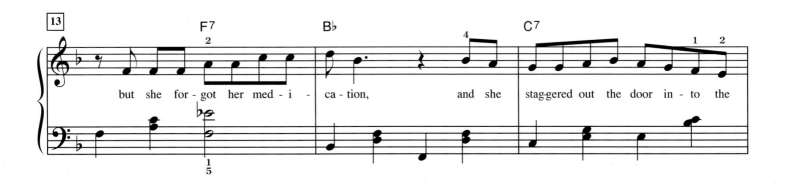

but she for-got her med-i-ca-tion, and she stag-gered out the door in-to the

snow. When we found her Christ-mas morn-ing

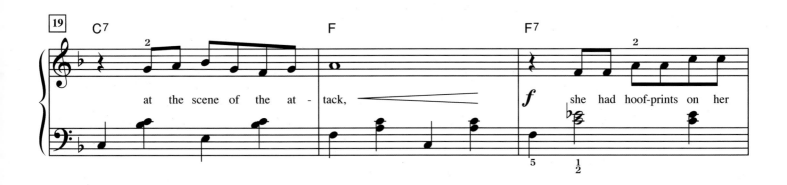

at the scene of the at-tack, she had hoof-prints on her

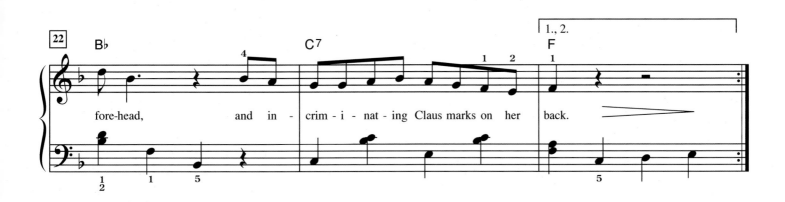

fore-head, and in-crim-i-nat-ing Claus marks on her back.

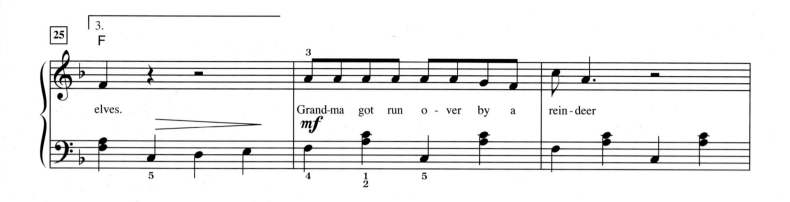

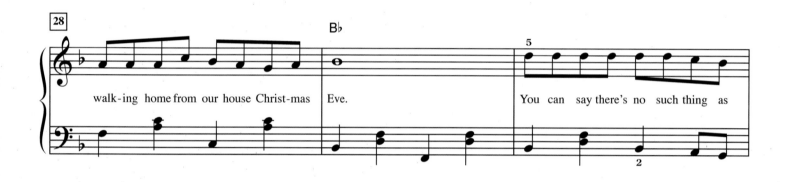

Verse 2:
Now we're all so proud of Grandpa,
He's been taking this so well.
See him in there watching football,
Drinking beer and playing cards with Cousin Mel.
It's not Christmas without Grandma.
All the family's dressed in black,
And we just can't help but wonder:
Should we open up her gifts or send them back?
(To Chorus:)

Verse 3:
Now the goose is on the table,
And the pudding made of fig,
And the blue and silver candles,
That would just have matched the hair in Grandma's wig.
I've warned all my friends and neighbors,
Better watch out for yourselves.
They should never give a licence
To a man who drives a sleigh and plays with elves.
(To Chorus:)

Have Yourself a Merry Little Christmas

Words and Music by
HUGH MARTIN and RALPH BLANE
Arranged by DAN COATES

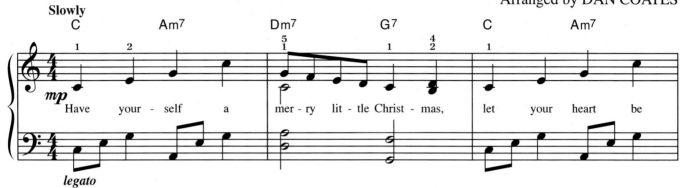

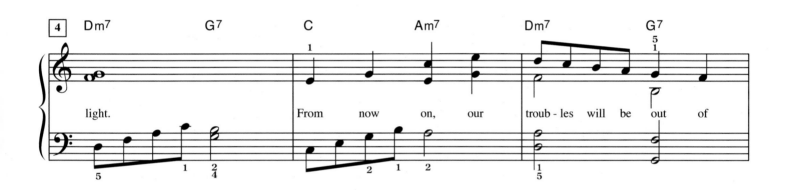

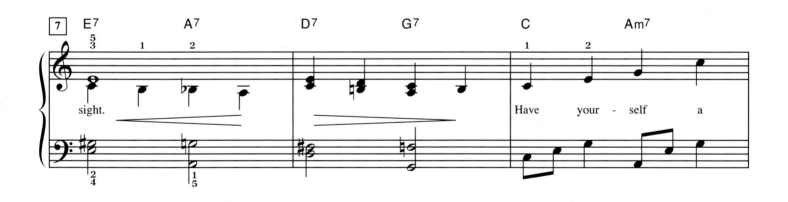

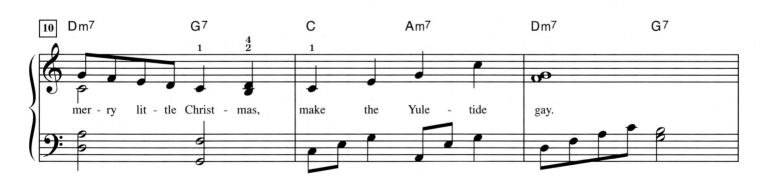

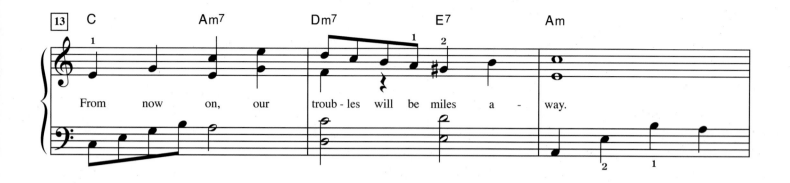

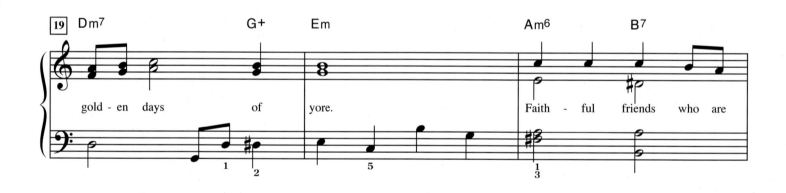

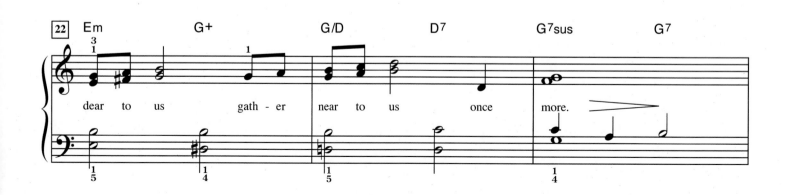

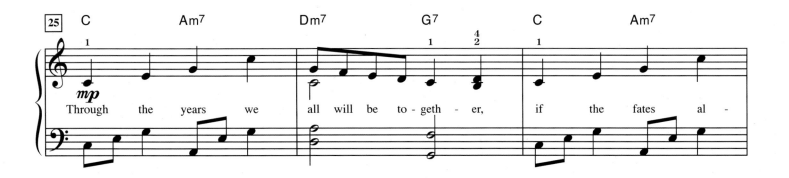

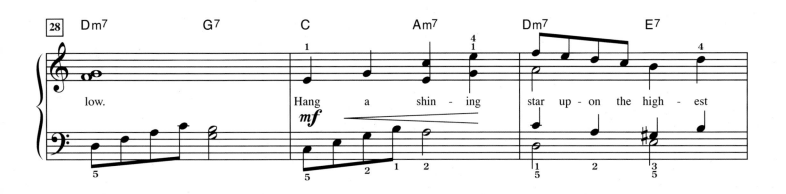

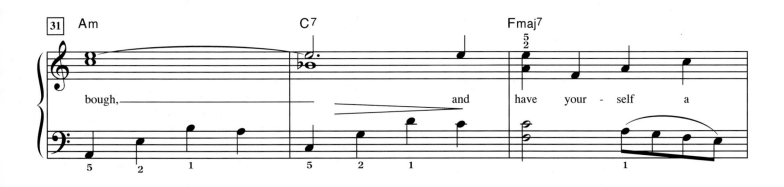

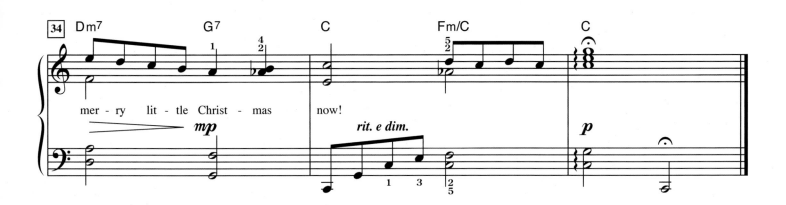

These Are the Special Times

Words and Music by
DIANE WARREN
Arranged by DAN COATES

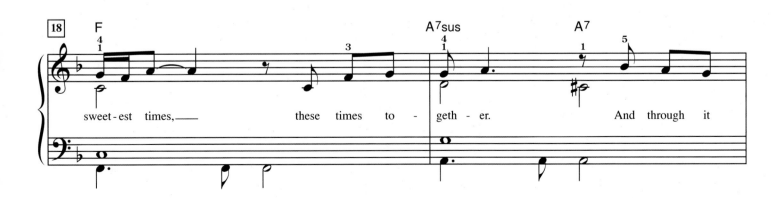

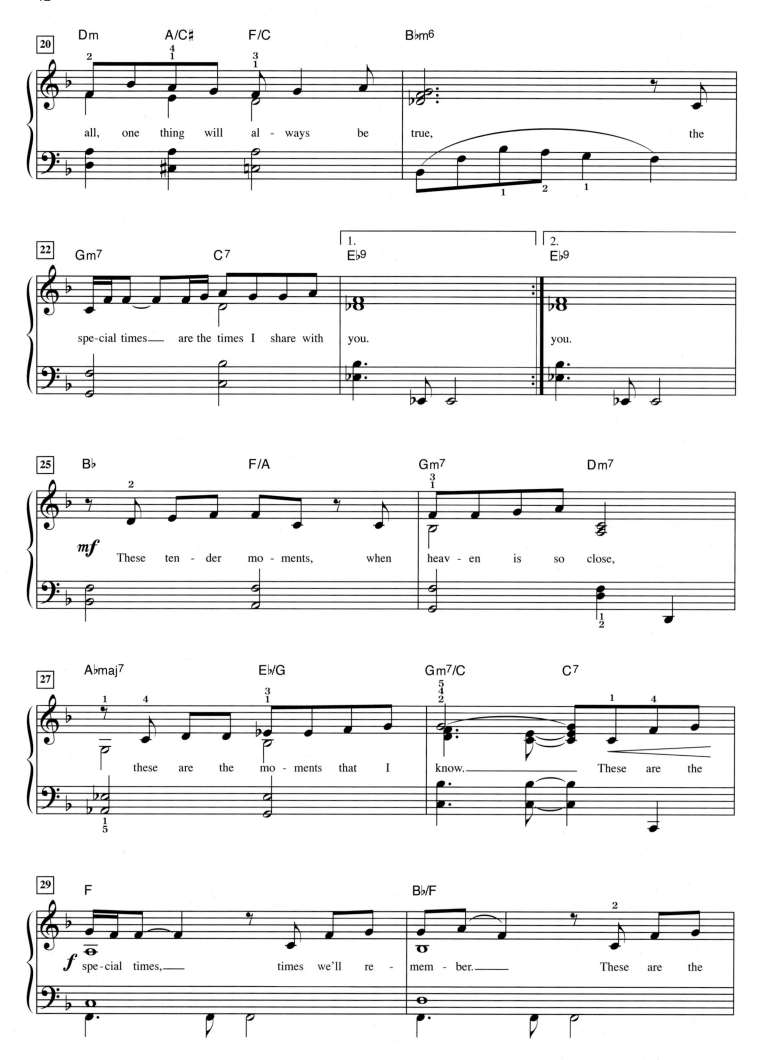

Christmas Mem'ries

Music by DON COSTA
Words by ALAN and MARILYN BERGMAN
Arranged by DAN COATES

Moderately slow

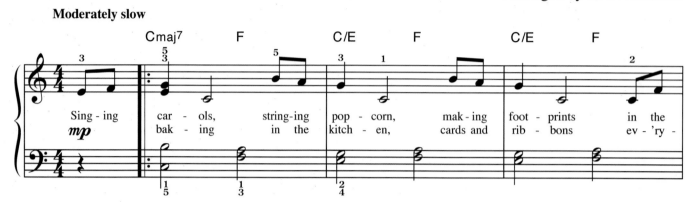

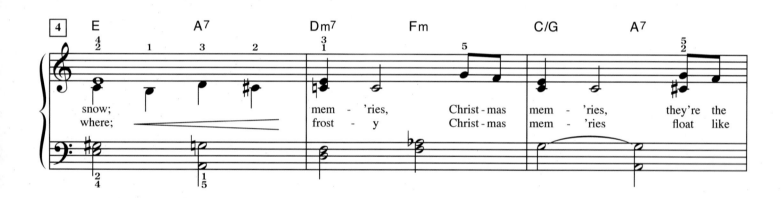

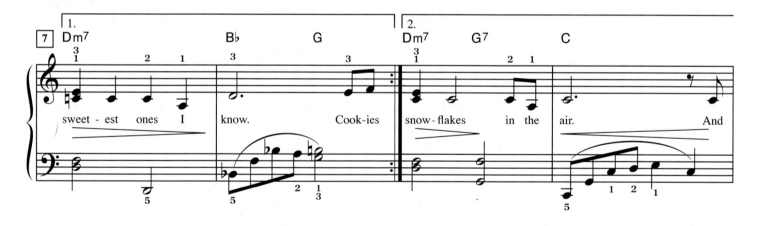

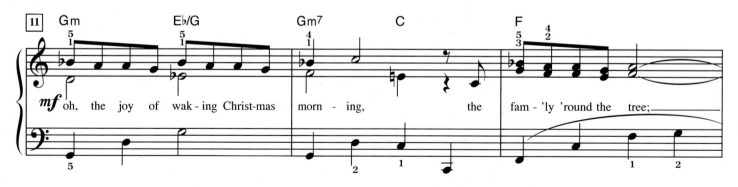

Winter Wonderland

Music by FELIX BERNARD
Words by DICK SMITH
Arranged by DAN COATES

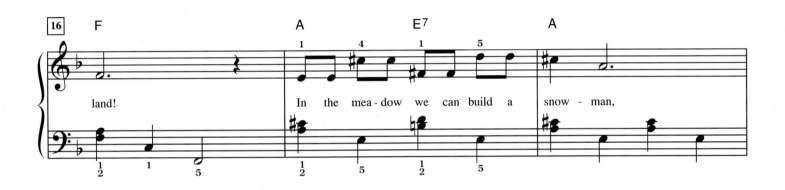

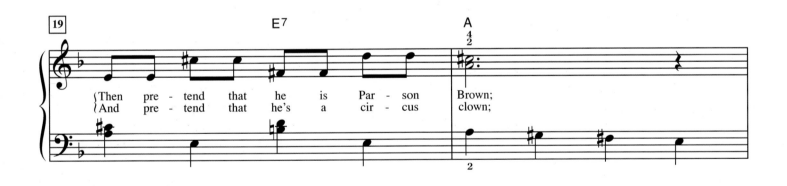

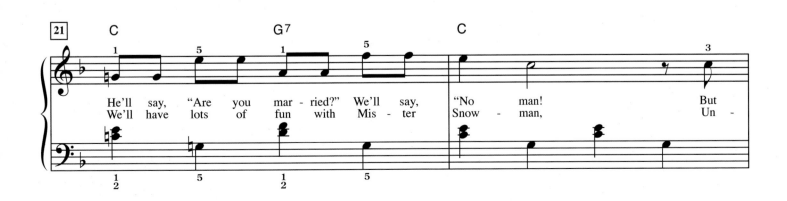

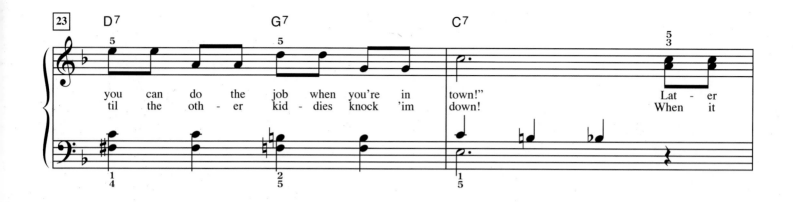

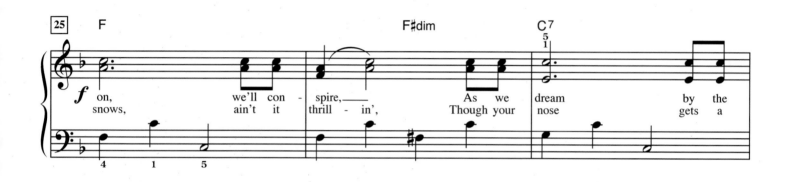

Grown-Up Christmas List

Words and Music by
DAVID FOSTER
and LINDA THOMPSON JENNER
Arranged by DAN COATES

Moderately slow

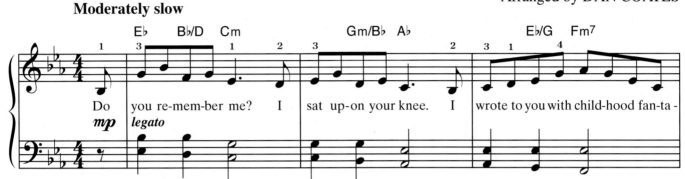

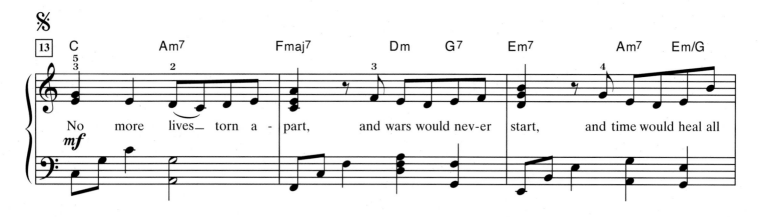

No more lives— torn a - part, and wars would nev-er start, and time would heal all

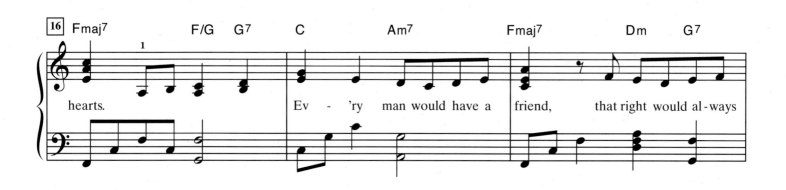

hearts. Ev - 'ry man would have a friend, that right would al-ways

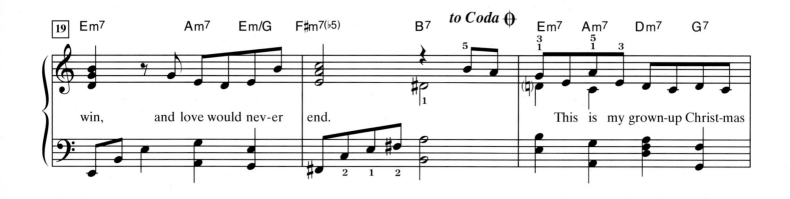

win, and love would nev-er end. This is my grown-up Christ-mas

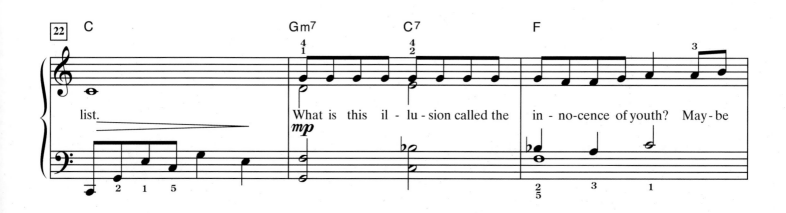

list. What is this il - lu - sion called the in - no-cence of youth? May-be

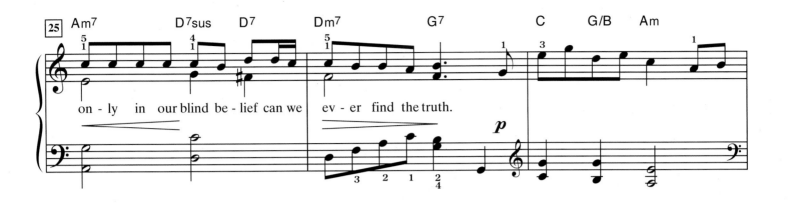

on - ly in our blind be - lief can we ev - er find the truth.

p

D. S. al Coda

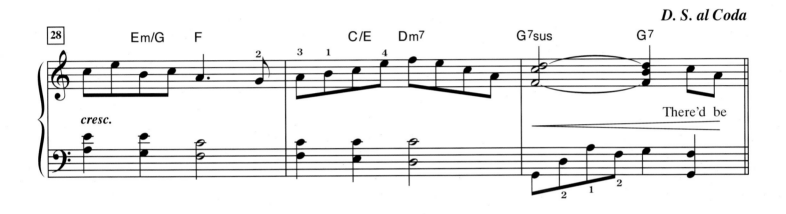

cresc.

There'd be

Coda

This is my grown-up Christ-mas list. This is my on - ly life-long wish. This is my grown-up Christ-mas

list.

mp

rit. e dim.

p

Do They Know It's Christmas?

Words and Music by Bob Geldof and Midge Ure
Arranged by DAN COATES

Moderately, with a steady beat

Sleigh Ride

Music by LEROY ANDERSON
Words by MITCHELL PARISH
Arranged by DAN COATES

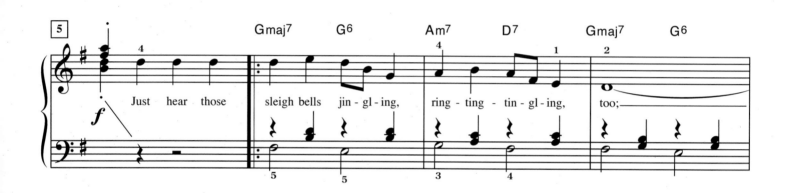

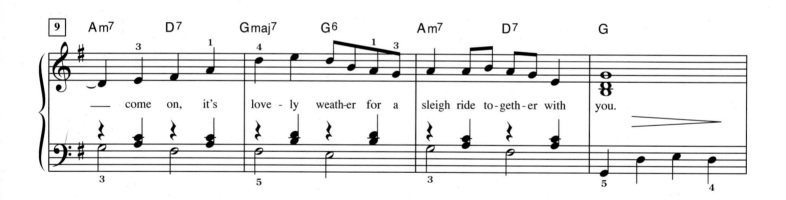

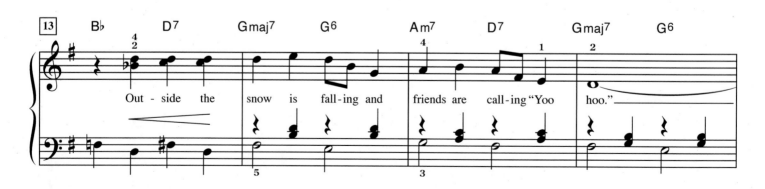

Believe

Words and Music by
GLEN BALLARD and ALAN SILVESTRI
Arranged by DAN COATES

You're a Mean One, Mr. Grinch

Music by ALBERT HAGUE
Lyric by DR. SEUSS
Arranged by DAN COATES

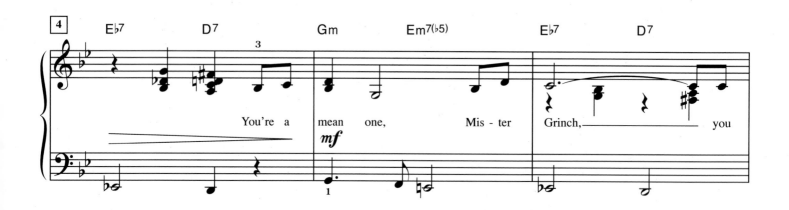

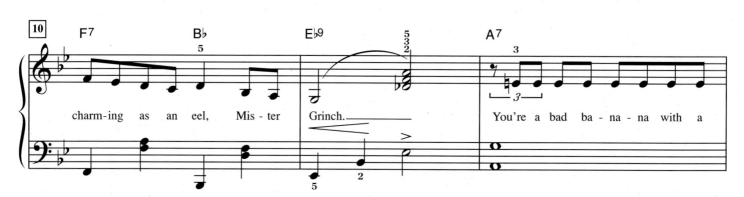